10
REASONS
WHY YOU ARE LIVING
CENTSLESS

A 10 Step Guide On Where You Are Spending Money
And How You Can Do Better

Ogechukwu Madu, MBA

Contents

Introduction

⊚⊚

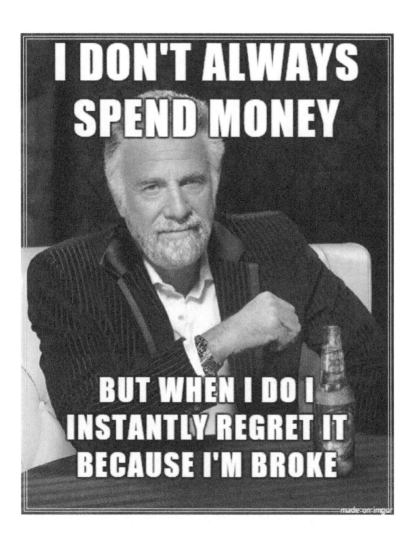

What does living "cents-less" mean?

Well first off, if you didn't get the pun, you should probably put down this book..or close whatever application you are reading this on.

Alright..Alright..I'm just kidding, you paid for this book, at the very least you can learn something right?!

Lesson 1: *Cents-less* is a play on words for the word *Senseless*.

(I can totally see the light bulbs turning on now)

Back to the original question.

What does living "cents-less" mean?

Simply? It means you don't have a great **understanding** of where you're **spending** your money.

The amount of money you have – or the lack there of - isn't as much of an issue as **where** you are actually spending the money you do have.

Let's think of a scenario:

You want to save money so that you can take a vacation to Cabo and enjoy some time away from "real life". You have 4 months to save up enough money, but you're finding it hard to save the specified amount.

Why is this?

Because your money has been **claimed** in other areas of your life that you probably wish it wasn't.

You must take a good look in the mirror and be **real** with yourself.

Spending money senselessly is only half of the problem.

The other half is your **mentality**.

There are an **abundant** amount of **millionaires** who make a great deal of money, but carelessly spend it and find it hard to save because they have continuously **rising** expenses.

It's crazy to think that someone can make a lot of money and still be living paycheck to paycheck.

Well you better believe it.

With the rise of **Social Media**, it is near impossible to not want to *"keep up with the Joneses"*

Which in turn leads to ...

(turn the page)

LIVING CENTSLESS!!

It's obvious with the purchase of this book that you are in need of *change.*

(another pun – haha)

Without further ado I welcome you to this 10 part, straight to the point guide – that if used **correctly** will help you make "cents" of where your money is going.

TO MAKE SENSE OF WHERE YOUR MONEY IS GOING, YOU MUST *EVALUATE* THE FOLLOWING 10 MONEY PITS OF YOUR FINANCIAL LIFE.

- Your **Residence**
- Your **Debt**
- Your **Ride**
- Your **Meals**

- Your **Budget**

- Your **Friends**

- Your **Wardrobe**

- Your **Upgrades**

- Your **Insurance**

- Your **Taxes**

Reason #1: Your Residence

Section 1*: King of the Bills*

Remember in the movie **Lion King,** Scar took over the Pride Lands and started **draining** the kingdom of its **resources** until it was a drought-stricken wasteland.

Guess what your rent is doing?

Draining your financial resources to the point that the other line items in your budget can't be adequately **sustained**.

If you were to only **focus** on lowering how much you spend on rent, you would be 3 times as likely to do these 3 things:

- 3 times as likely to tackle your car expenses.

- 3 times as likely to eat what you want each month.

- 3 times as likely to defeat debt.

Some of you may think,

"Well there's nothing I can't really do about the high rent. Paying 50%+ of my take-home income on rent is what goes with living in a big city."

Yes, this would be correct if your goal is to **continue** to be a cents-less fool.

But that's not your goal because you're reading this book to receive the much needed kick in the **gut** about where your money is going and learn tips that will enlighten you so that you no longer live cents-less.

Getting on your feet financially requires short-term **sacrifices** that are going to be hard to deal with.

This will **NOT BE EASY**!

It is **important** to understand that:

- You will not have to rent a room with someone in an apartment forever.

- You won't have to move in with your parents to avoid paying rent forever.

- You will not have to work multiple jobs forever.

The objective is to do what's needed to be done **today** so that you can do what you want **tomorrow**.

If you're currently paying **$1,300 a month** in rent, over **5 years** this becomes **$78,000** in rent paid to helping someone else be financially stable.

If you're in debt, especially **consumer debt**, why wouldn't you temporarily live in a place where you are paying a fraction of that amount, and use the difference to pay off your debt?

Just by living in a place where you are paying $1,000 a month would allow you to save **$300** which could be used to pay off debt or even save for a down payment on a home so that you never have to pay rent again.

Section 2: *Housing Costs*

Speaking of owning a home, let me give you the **411** on things you may not have considered when looking to buy a house.

You're not **truly** a homeowner, unless you have paid off the home in full.

Until then, consider yourself a **homeloaner**.

How you ask? Check this out.

You plan to take out a loan for a $180,000 home. Your **mortgage payment**, depending on how much you were able to contribute to a down payment, will be about $1,100 a month for 30 years. A $1,100 a month payment over 30 years is **$396,000**.

You wouldn't truly own the home until you paid **ATLEAST** $396,000 (that's over $100,000 in interest). Compare that to just **$180,000** if you already had the cash to buy the home outright.

A monthly mortgage isn't the only thing you should be worried about covering.

Other real estate costs to consider are:

Property Taxes: Every year your county performs an appraisal of the value of the home and assesses a tax in proportion to that value. So if your property is appraised at a higher value, you will see an increase in how much you pay in taxes.

PMI: Private Mortgage Insurance (PMI) is an insurance policy that protects the lender in the case you can't make your mortgage payments. The lender usually adds this insurance if you cannot afford a 20% down payment.

Annual Repairs: It's inevitable that you're going to have to repair something in your home. It can be a broken toilet, a faulty light switch or even replacing your ceiling fans.

Hazard or Flood Insurance: Hazard insurance covers unintentional damage by fire, smoke, wind, hail and other similar events. It is separate from flood insurance, which may be required if your home is located in a floodplain.

Home Warranty: This is a contract that provides discounted services on a home's major components such as the furnace, air conditioning, plumbing, etc.

HOA Fees: If the home you purchased is located in a gated community or leased land property, you are required to join the communities Homeowners Association (HOA) and pay a monthly, quarterly, or annual fee which is used for the upkeep of the common areas of the community.

Security System: It is important to feel protected. You may feel the need to install a security system to protect yourself from intruders. There is usually a monthly fee to have this service.

Utilities: Most home utilities include, electricity, water and sewer, and heating. These costs can fluctuate depending on the time of the year.

Total these above expenses and come up with a **monthly average** before comparing buying a home to your rent payment.

This allows you to find out what you can **comfortably** afford to spend a month.

Conclusion:

Here's how to be "Cents-ible" with your money if renting

If you're in your early 20's and do not have any dependents, living in a **low-cost fashion** will be easier now than later in your life. It would be cents-ible to capitalize on this.

You can minimize rent expenses by:

- **Living with relatives**: If this scenario is feasible, this is an easy way to keep rent cost to a minimum.

- **Share a rental with roommates**: You have to give up some privacy, but this is a great option to keep rent expenses low.

- **Move to a cheaper rental**: If you're currently are living above your means and you don't want to live with roommates - this maybe the option for you.

- **Negotiate rental increases**: If you're a good tenant, you may be able to talk your landlord into lowering the increased price when it's time to re-sign the lease.

Here's how to be "Cents-ible" with your money if you have a house

If you're a homeowner or about to become one, use these steps to keep your ownership costs under control.

- **Buy a house that you can afford**: Even if you can afford the monthly mortgage payments, if you have too little money left for your other needs and wants, your home may become a financial prison.

Keep your total monthly real estate expenses below 33% of your total household income.

- **Get a Roommate**: Owning the home becomes much more affordable if you have monthly rental income coming in from renting out a bedroom.

- **Avoid Adjustable Interest Rates**: DO NOT accept any type of adjustable rate mortgage or interest only mortgage as there is a high possibility of the interest rates increasing, leaving you with uncontrollable monthly payments.

Reason #2: Your Debt

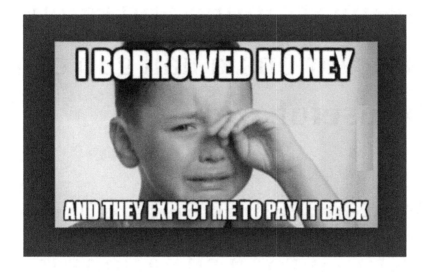

Taking on debt and borrowing money is like using a **nail gun**. With proper training and safety precautions, a nail gun can be **useful**.

When used improperly or in the wrong situations it can cause **serious damage**.

The same can be said with borrowing money. If used cents-ibly, loans can **help** you accomplish important goals and boost your net worth over time, but…….

The reason you are probably reading this book is because you **weren't** sensible with the money you've borrowed and now you're:

- living beyond your **means**

- borrowing against future earnings &

- lowering your long term net worth.

Section 1: *Understanding Debt*

Not all debt is **bad**. Yes, I said it.

Borrowing money for things that will give you **opportunities** to generate even more money makes financial sense.

Taking on debt for your schooling, buying a business or purchasing real estate can give you a **return** on your investment.

Taking on debt for things like a new car, new furniture, or a costly vacation makes zero "cents" ...literally.

Section 2: *Consumer Debt*

You accumulate consumer debt (credit cards, car loans, etc) when your expenses **exceed** your income.

Therefore, it only makes sense that to pay off consumer debt, you will need to **decrease** your spending and/or increase your income. (preferably "and" instead of "or")

This section will help you jumpstart getting rid of consumer debt.

How to get rid of consumer debt:

1) **Kick the credit card habit:** If you have been in the habit of accumulating debt on credit cards, you better cut up your credit cards and cancel your accounts, **IMMEDIATELY**.

Like right now.

You don't need the temptation. You can manage your finances and expenses without having a credit card.

2) **There's this thing called a debit card**: Getting rid of your credit card doesn't mean you have to start carrying large amounts of cash around wherever you go.

There are three major differences between a credit card and a debit card.

- With a debit card your money gets deducted from your checking account immediately. You are spending your own money instead of the banks.

- With a debit card it is possible to overdraw your checking account. This means the bank will charge you for spending money that wasn't in your account.

Make sure to receive **alerts** when funds get low.

- With a debit card you usually have a **week** to dispute fraudulent charges compared to a credit card where you could have up to **60 days** to dispute a charge.

3) **Use savings and investments to reduce debt:** If you happen to have savings or investment balances that **could** pay off high interest credit card debt or car loans **DO IT**.

Just leave enough cash to withstand any unexpected large expenses.

Your investments may be **earning** a decent return, but if your credit card loans are accumulating at a 15% interest rate it's **wise** to pay that off first.

Why?

Because your investments would need to be making returns of over 21% (if you're in a moderate tax bracket) to net 15% after paying taxes to justify keeping your high interest consumer debt.

Example:

You have $9,000 in savings, and the bank is paying you 1%. (You would have $9,090 at the end of the year)

You also have $7,000 in consumer debt that is collecting 10% interest (you owe $7,700 at the end of the year).

It is wise to pay off the consumer debt because you have guaranteed yourself 10% interest that you will keep in your pocket.

Lets say you didn't pay off the debt in full. By the end of the year you have technically lost $610 ($9,090 − $7,700 = 1,390).

If you have paid the consumer debt off at the beginning of the year, your balance would be $2,000 ($9,000 – $7,000 = $2,000).

$2000 - $1390 = $610 in lost revenue.

Conclusion:

How to "Cents-ibly" prevent consumer debt

The following list will highlight tactics you can use to limit the influence that credit cards and consumer debt hold over your life:

- **Replace your credit card with a debit card:** Provides convenience without credit temptation.

- **Think in terms of total cost:** Everything sounds cheaper in terms of monthly payments. That's how salesmen get you to buy things you can't afford.

Use the calculator on your phone and add up the total expenses. That should scare you into not buying things you can't afford.

- **Go shopping without a card or check:** Just bring a small amount of cash with you and you can't overspend.

- **Get help:** If you know that you have a spending addiction, look for professional help to overcome it.

Reason #3: Your Ride

⊚⊚

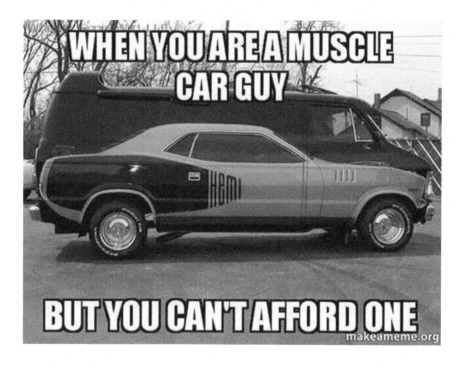

Section 1: *The real cost of getting around town*

You really want to see how cents-less you have been? Let's look into what your car is **really** costing you per month.

The real cost to own an average car:

Car Note:	$400 a month
Insurance:	$110 a month
Gas:	$175 a month
Depreciation*:	$85 a month
Maintenance & Repairs:	$90 a month
Total:	$860 a month

*The typical $18,000 car will be worth about $5,000 less in 5 years

The real cost to own an average **luxury** car:

Car Note:	$575 a month
Insurance:	$150 a month
Gas:	$225 a month
Depreciation*:	$235 a month
Maintenance & Repairs:	$255 a month
Total:	$1,440 a month

*Typical $35,000 car will be worth $14,000 less in 5 years.

Besides the amount of money spent, can you tell what the chief **difference** is between both car owners?

Not

A

Damn

Thing

Let's put this into even more perspective.

Your take home pay is **$2,500 a month.**

Your rent is **$1,200 a month.**

What you are REALLY paying towards your car is closer to **$900 a month.**

Riddle me this.

How the heck are you going to pay for:

- Food

- Cell phone*

- Utilities

- Credit card balance

- Student loan payments

And **anything else** with a total of $400?!

*Somehow this always gets paid, go figure.

You're not.

Let me tell you what's more than **likely** going to happen.

You are still living in LaLa Land and think your car payments are about the typical $500 a month. So you're going to fill the remainder of your budget with expenditures you already can't afford.

Guess what happens next?

I. Your oil change light comes on.

II. You get a nail in your tire that can't get patched for **free** at Discount Tire.

III. It's that time to **renew** your registration / inspection sticker.

You don't know what to do, but now you learn that a payday loan shop will loan you the money.

Now you have loan sharks after you because you **definitely** couldn't make those payments.

(That can't possibly end well)

Here are some **guidelines** to follow that can save you future headaches when purchasing a vehicle:

- **Price:** Try to keep the price under $12,000 (tax and license included) and pay for it in cash.

- **Reliability:** Toyota, Honda, or Nissan. (these have proven reliability)

- **Age:** Car should be 2 years and older.

- **Mileage:** 15,000 miles for every year the vehicle is old (a 5 year car you are wanting to buy should not have more than 75,000 miles)

- **Inspection:** Don't worry about the warranty. Negotiate the car to be inspected before the purchase.

By following those guidelines, you will find that the average of what you are **paying** a month become:

Car **PAYMENT**:	$200 a month
Insurance:	$90 a month
Gas:	$160 a month
Depreciation:	$50 a month
Maintenance & Repairs:	$100 a month
Total:	$600 a month

"*Wait!*" Some of you say. "*Why is the car payment $200 a month when I already bought the car with cash?*"

Because as long as you **own** a car you **will** have car payments, but you will never have a **car note**.

Instead of paying back a loan of $200 a month, pay yourself the $200 and in 5 years you will have **$12,000** for use toward an updated vehicle.

Section 2: *Financing*

Obviously, there are going to people who will convince themselves into **needing** to take out a loan for a car.

Sigh..

The following is what those people should **aim** to do since they obviously love defying me.

Follow the same guidelines stated previously on purchasing a vehicle (buying under 12k, making sure it's reliable, etc)

Request a loan with a credit union before getting heckled by the car dealership finance team.

You shouldn't pay more than 6% APR* for a loan on a $12,000 vehicle. If your credit report is bad, you can put half down and convince the financier to bring the APR down to around 10%.

If the financier says nothing under 21% then you most likely can't afford the payments and should **leave**.

Accepting any loan with over **20% interest** is living cents-less.

If you happen to get approved at a credit union, use it as a **bargaining chip** to get a better price on the vehicle you are trying to purchase. Take the vehicle for an inspection to make sure there isn't anything wrong with it.

Lastly, pay the vehicle off as **fast** as you can!

*APR or Annual Percentage Rate: The yearly cost of a loan, including interest, insurance, and the origination fee (points), expressed as a percentage. Often applied to mortgages, credit cards, and automobile financing.

Conclusion:

How to be "Cents-ible" with your money by trimming transportation expenses

Here are some suggestions that can help you control your transportation costs.

- **Choose Public Transportation:** If you live in an area that offers reliable public transportation such as a subway or a bus system, take advantage of the monthly passes.

- **Ride your bike:** This includes motorcycles! During warmer months consider this as a means of getting around.

- **If having a car is a must, go cheap and reliable:** The main reason why people spend more than they can afford on a car is because they finance the purchase. When buying a car you should buy one with cash, which for most people means a good-quality used car.

Reason #4: Your Meals

Spending money on food like

Section 1: *Health is Wealth*

I'm sure you have heard of the saying "Health is Wealth". Health is indeed wealth in its own fashion because there is no reason to **pursue** building wealth if you're not going to be active enough to enjoy it.

There is an **epidemic** in the United States where the majority of people are living to eat instead of eating to live.

If you're living to eat, guess what you are doing?

Cents-lessly spending your money!

The average **obese** American man can expect to spend an **additional** $1,200 a year in medical costs.

The average obese American woman should expect to spend **an extra** $3,800 a year in the same category.

I'm not even **factoring** in costs from being overweight - bigger clothes, extra seat ticket when flying, etc.

Some of you reading this book are thinking to yourselves

"I'm not obese, I don't have to worry about those costs."

Sure, you might not be overweight, but you're mostly likely going **over budget** on your food expenses.

How do I know?

I would probably cash in on a bet that **90%** of you reading this book do not budget for food.

There are a significant number of people that use the "**pay and pray**" method nowadays.

They are too scared to check the bank account before **paying** for that fast food meal, and **pray** that they don't hear, "your card has been declined".

If this is you, **acknowledge** it. The only way to change is the admission of a problem.

Ok, so there are some of you who actually **DO** budget for food.

Do you **typically** do the following?

If you're single no kids: Budget $450 for the month (but spend closer to $600)

If you have a family with kids: Budget $650 for the month (but spend close to $900)

Thank Goodness you picked up this book. Go to the next page to see how to improve.

How To Improve:

There are three major categories that apply to what is spent on food.

- **Groceries**: Set an amount that you CAN NOT go over (i.e. $150) & **pay in CASH.**

- **Dining Out**: Set a daily limit that WILL NOT go over (i.e. $7/a day Mon-Thurs and $10/ a day Fri - Sun) & **pay in CASH.**

- **Entertainment:** Set a monthly amount for weekly special occasions, like going out to eat with the family. (i.e. $100 a month or $25 a week) & **pay in CASH.**

This method is similar to calorie tracking; it allows you to become more **AWARE** of what you are spending on food.

Conclusion:

How to "Cents-ibly" manage food cost

The following will help with food expenses and could even improve your health!

- **Learn how to cook:** Take a course and read some good books or articles on cooking. If you don't know how to cook for yourself and how to do so healthfully, you will end up spending a lot more money on fast food which really isn't good for your belly or your wallet.

- **Consider store brands:** The main reason you spend money on higher priced items is because companies usually spend more in advertising and marketing. You can save a considerable amount of money by purchasing the store brand versus the name brand.

- **Buy in bulk:** Buying in bulk from the likes of Sam's Club and Costco can be helpful in saving money, but be mindful when buying items that can spoil. You are wasting money if you don't consume the items before they expire.

- **Pack your lunch:** Eating out everyday gets expensive. This is why you should learn how to cook.

- **Be mindful when dining out:** It's more cost efficient to eat out for breakfast or lunch rather than dinner. You usually will get more "bang for your buck" at those times. Also, drink water instead of carbonated drinks and alcohol as those costs really add up.

Reason #5: Your Budget

Section 1: *Blown Budget*

I can hear the complaints now...

"Budgeting sucks"

"It never works for me"

"I constantly go over budget"

Hmm...

Guess what I have to say to those complaints...

TOO

BAD

Do you know what is **worse** than putting in some time and effort into **creating** a REALISTIC budget?

The fact that you're going to **stay** living cents-less, which will eventually lead you to becoming **broke**.

You already **know** how living cents-less is.

You spend until there is **no** money left.

No wait—you realize you can still spend the **bank's money** so you max out your credit cards.

Can't use credit cards anymore? Well there's a payday loan shop down the street **ready** for your business.

Let's cut the crap!

If you want to change your financial status, you must put in the work.

I'm going to discuss some smart budgeting strategies.

Have your pen and paper ready.

Step 1: List all of your current monthly expenses on **paper**. And yes, it must be on paper; it sinks in better this way.

- Make sure to total infrequent expenses that happen throughout the year. (vacation, Christmas gifts, etc). Take that total and divide it by 12 to get the monthly average.

Step 2: Create a **Goal** column next to your current written expenses.

Step 3: Go through your current expenses and **find** things to cut back on so that you can find money you can **apply** toward your financial goals (buying a house, pay off debts, etc).

- Write the new lower numbers in the goal column, so you can compare.

Step 4: Open a **separate** checking account just for spending and keep your primary checking for bills. This allows you to direct deposit a percentage of your check into both checking accounts.

Here's an example of some **items** that should be **paid** for with your spending account.

- Bills
- Restaurants
- Groceries
- Clothing
- Any entertainment
- Any online shopping purchases

Step 5: Open an account with Mint or Quicken and keep yourself on track.

- Mint is a great FREE personal finance tracking software that allows you to see all of your checking, savings, investing, and loan accounts in one place. This is BIG TIME!

I'll let you all in on my budget percentages as I am sure you may be curious.

I have 5 different accounts that I direct deposit my money into (I am not including my retirement accounts).

Below are my percentages:

- **Necessities (60%):** I currently put 60% of my income into this checking account. I use this account to pay my mortgage, food, gas, bills, etc.

- **Long Term Savings (10%):** This is for big-ticket items or investments I want to pay for in a year or beyond.

- **Play (10%):** This is for leisurely expenses such as movies, sporting events, pretty much anything regarding entertainment. I spend all of the money in this account every month.

- **Education (10%):** This is for books, courses, seminars, mentoring and more currently paying off graduate school loans. It is important that I continually educate myself.

- **Investing (10%):** This goes directly into a brokerage account. I use the money at the end of the month to purchase stocks or funds.

When setting your budget it's important not to overthink the details and believe in your ability to stick to it.

It's all in your mindset so stop making excuses and just do it.

Reason #6: Your Friends

◎◎

Section 1: *Spend Pals*

Some **rich** guy said we are the **average** of the **five people** we spend the **most time with**.

Take a second and think about your **closest** friends.

Are they living cents-less?

(you may want to buy them this book as a temporary goodbye present when you understand you have to get serious and cut the crap to get where you want financially.)

It's hard to **save or spend** your money **wisely** when the people closest to you encourage you to do otherwise.

Maybe your friends don't fall into this category. That's **fantastic** – you can ignore this section.

But if you are **REAL** with yourself and realize that

you do have these kinds of friends...

PAY ATTENTION!!!

If your goal is to stop being so cents-less with your money, you're going to have to **temporarily** remove yourself from as many financially **negative influences** as possible.

Who falls under this category?

- Friends who **know** they are financially cents-less and continue to spend with no regard because..."YOLO!"

- Friends who literally don't know how bad they are with money, but **think** they are in pretty good shape.

- Family or even romantic partners who **expect the world** from you financially.

As I mentioned before, the **extraction** of yourself from these friends are only temporary until you get your finances in **order**.

Hopefully when you reach this point, you would be able to return to them and **teach by example** because you now have a leg to stand on.

If that doesn't work — time to cut them off forever. Their loss not yours.

Conclusion:

Here's how to "Cents-ibly" keep relationships

- **Audit your inner circle:** By evaluating your friends, you can save yourself a lifetime of pain and regret. Temporary extraction from them can bring a positive effect toward your financial goals.

- **Do not loan friends or family money:** If you care about a friendship or relationship, lending the person a significant amount of money will change that. Once you get started on this path, you will become an enabler instead of a friend.

Reason #7: Your Wardrobe

⊚⊚

Section 1: *Fashion Statement*

We value brands **way more** than we should. It's hard not to especially if you watch TV or are on social media. It is a company's **job** to sell you on the perception of their brand.

But we must **change** the level of value placed on the material things that we are constantly bombarded with.

Remember:

You are not your **Rolex watch**.

You are not your **Louboutin heels**.

You are not your **Ralph Lauren Polo**.

Conclusion:

How to "Cents-ibly" finesse your fashion finances

Here's how to look like a million bucks without spending it.

- Buy **quality** items only. This includes name brands – just do a little research before purchasing.

- Use the items that you purchase for **long periods** of time. Pick items that mesh well with other items or colors.

- If it's in your closet and you haven't **used** or **thought** about it for **six months**, donate it. (You can claim the deduction when you file taxes.)

- Don't **chase** the latest fashion. True fashion changes slowly and classics never really go out of style.

- Stay away from clothes that need **dry cleaning**. Money Pits.

- Buy **gently used** clothing at vintage shops. You can find name brand clothing for a fraction of the cost.

- Look for major **discounts**. Many stores have major sales once or twice a year. Figure out when it will happen at the places that sell your favorite brands.

Reason #8: Your Upgrade

◎◎

Section 1: *Latest & Greatest*

Look at your phone. Is it the latest and greatest iPhone or Android?

The answer is probably **yes.**

What's worse is that compared to the previous model, there usually isn't a feature added that truly **justifies** the need for an upgrade.

So why do you continue to upgrade?

One Word:

Hyperconsumption

(The consumption of goods for non-functional purposes and the associated significant pressure to goods exerted by the modern capitalist society.)

People constantly **upgrade** their possessions while **downgrading** their quality of life.

Think about it.

Let's take Twitter for example. How many times have you seen someone post a picture of themselves with the newest iPhone and a Louis Vuitton bag nearby, but their mattress is on the floor with no bedding?

Priorities, People...

Priorities!

Conclusion:

How to "Cents-ibly" upgrade

- **Use the "trading places" method for significant purchases**: before you buy a big-ticket item, find something around your home to sell or trade on online platforms like eBay or Facebook Messenger.

- **Limit ad exposure**: Stop consuming so much irrelevant information such as consumer ads though TV's and the Internet.

Reason #9: Your Insurance

◎◎

"Since you have a brick house, your huffing and puffing rates are way down."

Section 1: *Why Insurance?*

Insurance (Car, House, Renters, Health, etc) can **make** or **break** you financially.

Obviously no one likes to pay their **hard-earned** money to an insurance company.

But if you end up in a car accident or if someone breaks into your home and takes all of your valuables, you will be extremely **unhappy** if you didn't have the proper insurance and had to pay for **everything** out of pocket.

I would know – back in my college days I had a break-in at my apartment and I did not have **renters' insurance**.

The bastards took **ALL** of my electronics.

As you can imagine, I was not happy having to **start all over** and buy things like a laptop and a TV again.

The point is, if you want to live life on the edge by not having any insurance, don't expect anyone to contribute to your **GoFundMe** post when an "emergency" happens.

Section 2: *Protecting your home and possessions*

When you buy a home, the mortgage lender **requires** you to get homeowners insurance.

Why?

Because like you, the lender wants to **protect** their investment in the property (the money lent to you to buy the home).

If you are still renting, it is **wise** to look at the renters insurance for the same reason.

When buying a homeowners policy, seek out coverage that includes a "**guaranteed replacement cost**". This insures that if a fire burns down your house you'd have enough money to rebuild the home.

If you own a condo or are a renter, you need to select a **personal property coverage** that you believe will cover the cost of replacing all of your personal items.

Section 3: *Insuring your car*

Cars are **money pits**, but depending on your location you need one to get around.

Accidents are almost **inescapable** and having the right auto insurance will provide **liability protection**.

Liability protection comes in different forms. The two main ones are:

- **Bodily injury liability:** Covers injury to people. If purchasing, it would be wise to get one that covers twice the value of your assets.

- **Property damage liability:** Covers damage to property, including cars. Coverage of $50,000 is a good minimum.

Conclusion:

Here's how to be less "cents-less"

The following tips can help you **minimize** your insurance spending while making the most of it.

- Utilize **high** deductibles. A deductible is how much you have to pay before the insurance policy **kicks in**. The higher the deductible, the **lower** the premium (how much you have to pay a month).

- Don't buy insurance for anything that won't be financially **catastrophic** if you have to pay for it out of your own pocket.

• Rates vary among insurers. **Always** shop around for the best price.

• Take care of your health; you have only one body and one shot to take care of it.

Reason #10: Your Taxes

This is the chapter where your eyes will probably start to glaze over but I'll try to make it as painless as possible.

Many people don't realize that along with your housing costs, taxes are most likely one of your biggest expenses.

With taxes being such a large expense, you should become very motivated to do what you can to reduce them, RIGHT?!

This section will help you understand what strategies you can use to reduce your income taxes.

Section 1: *Understanding Taxable Income*

Taxable income is any type of compensation that triggers a tax liability.

There are two different type of taxable income:

- **Earned Income**, which can include wages, salary, bonuses, tips, etc.

- **Unearned Income**, which can include dividends, interest, earnings, royalties, etc.

To **understand** how taxable income is **calculated**, let's look at the following scenario:

In 2017, your adjusted income is **$40,000**. If you're **married** and have **two kids**, this is how you're your taxable income would be tabulated.

*Taxable income = adjusted income – (deductions + allowance for exemptions)

Taxable income = $40,000 – ($12,700 + $4,050 x 2)

Taxable income = $40,000 – ($12,700 + $8,100)

Taxable income = $40,000 – $20,800

Taxable income = $19,200

Use this number in the next section to see how much you would be paying it taxes.

*In 2017, the amount for standard deductions for a married couple is 12,700. The standard exemption is $4,050 per kid.

Section 2: *Understanding Tax Rates*

Not **all** income is treated **equally**!

If you earn a **constant** salary throughout the course of a year, an equal amount of federal and state taxes are usually **deducted** from each paycheck.

Therefore, you are probably **thinking** that all of your earned income is being taxed equally.

This is not the case.

What really happens is you are paying **less tax** on the money **earned from the beginning of the year** and **more** on **earned income** at the **end** of the year.

How? Well I'll show you.

If you are **single** and your taxable income totals $50,000 during 2017, you will pay **federal tax** at the rate of **10%** on the **first** $9,325 of taxable income

15% on the income between $9,325 and $37,950, and

25% on income from $37,950 to $91,900.

Your **tax rate** would be **25%** according to the 2017 Tax Bracket Table below.

Single

Rate	Taxable Income Bracket	Tax Owed
10%	$0 to $9,325	10% of Taxable Income
15%	$9,325 to $37,950	$932.50 plus 15% of the excess over $9325
25%	$37,950 to $91,900	$5,226.25 plus 25% of the excess over $37,950
28%	$91,900 to $191,650	$18,713.75 plus 28% of the excess over $91,900
33%	$191,650 to $416,700	$46,643.75 plus 33% of the excess over $191,650
35%	$416,700 to $418,400	$120,910.25 plus 35% of the excess over $416,700
39.60%	$418,400+	$121,505.25 plus 39.6% of the excess over $418,400

Married filing jointly

Rate	Taxable Income Bracket	Tax Owed
10%	$0 to $18,650	10% of taxable income
15%	$18,650 to $75,900	$1,865 plus 15% of the excess over $18,650
25%	$75,900 to $153,100	$10,452.50 plus 25% of the excess over $75,900
28%	$153,100 to $233,350	$29,752.50 plus 28% of the excess over $153,100
33%	$233,350 to $416,700	$52,222.50 plus 33% of the excess over $233,350
35%	$416,700 to $470,700	$112,728 plus 35% of the excess over $416,700
39.60%	$470,700+	$131,628 plus 39.6% of the excess over $470,700

Section 3: *Ways to reduce taxes on employment income*

Here are some **legal** ways to reduce your income taxes on work-related income:

- **Funding a retirement plan:** You can omit money from your taxable income by funding an employer-based retirement plan such as a 401k or 403b account or self-employed plans such as SEP-IRAs.

Not only do these options reduce your taxes, they also help build a **nest egg** that you won't need to touch until later in life.

Many people miss out on this great opportunity for reducing taxes because they **spend** almost all of their current employment income and have **hardly** anything left to put into a retirement account.

If this sounds like you, you need to reduce your spending or increase your income without increasing spending, so that you will be able to **contribute** to your retirement plan.

One thing I do is have money taken out of my paycheck **automatically** and direct deposited into my 401k, so I don't get **tempted** to spend the money elsewhere.

- **Using health savings accounts:** A Health Savings Account (HSA) allows you to store money away for **future** medical expenses. The benefit of having this account besides the tax savings is you can **withdraw** money from a HSA tax-free so long as the money is used for healthcare costs.

Retirement accounts can't even offer this!

- **Self Employment Deductions:** When you are self-employed, basic things like portions of your cell phone bill or car mileage can be **deducted** when calculating the tax you owe.

It's a shame how many self-employed people **do not** take **advantage** of the many deductions they qualify for.

In most cases, people just aren't **aware** of what they can deduct or they are worried that large deductions will **increase their risk** of being audited.

My recommendation is hire **qualified tax help** and **keep** a record of everything.

Bookkeeping is essential!

Section 4: *Education Tax Breaks*

American tax laws provide several tax reduction opportunities for education related expenses. Here are a few to consider:

- **Tax deductions for college expenses:** The tuition and fees deduction can reduce the amount of your income subject to tax by up to $4,000. This deduction, reported on **Form 8917**, Tuition and Fees Deduction, is taken as an adjustment to income.

- **Tax free investment earnings:** Money invested in a Section 529 plan is sheltered from taxation and **is not taxed** upon withdrawal if the money is used for educational expenses. Depending on the state you live in you can contribute up to $380,000 in a 529 plan.

- **Tax credits:** The American Opportunity and Lifetime Learning credits provide **tax relief** to low and moderate- income earners facing education costs. The full credit (up to $2,500) is available to individuals whose gross income is $80,000 or less.

Conclusion:

How to make "cents" of your taxes:

Utilize these tips to help reduce your taxes.

Exploit retirement savings plans: To take advantage of such plans, you must spend less than you earn. Only then can you afford to contribute to these plans.

Reduce the amount of sales tax you pay: When you buy most consumer products, you pay sales tax. Therefore, if you spend less money and save more in retirement accounts, you reduce your income and sales taxes.

Buy and Hold: When you buy growth investments such as stocks or real estate, you should **hold** on to them for the long term -

depending on the circumstances of course.

The government rewards your patience with lower tax rates on your profits.

So for example if you were to own stock for over a year and you're in the 25% tax rate bracket ($37,950-$91,900), you will only have to pay 15% on the long term gains made from the stock.

What's Next?

⊙⊙

"We talked about this. Stop spending money like this."

Thank you for taking the time to read this book. I hope you have learned at least one thing that you either didn't know about or were refreshed on. Hopefully you will encourage your friends and family to read this gem as well!

The idea of this writing was to go back to the basics and bring to light where exactly you're spending your hard-earned money. Some of you consider yourselves to be pretty good savers. I did as well. But, I learned that once you account for where your money is really going, that allows you to save more money

for one particular
purpose...

TO

INVEST!

In a future book, I will provide more detailed information but for now, know that using the methods learned in this book to stop **"living cent-less"** means nothing if you're not finding ways to make your money grow.

You must learn to invest, whether through the stock market, real estate, or even a small business.

So once again thank you, and enjoy your newfound commitment to no longer LIVING CENTSLESS!

Made in the USA
Middletown, DE
27 March 2020

87346887R10116